Would

Book for Kids

A 700 Hilarious, Funny, Silly, Easy, Hard and Challenging Question Game Fun for Family, Teens and Children

Funny Fox

TABLE OF CONTENTS

INTRODUCTION

We would like to personally thank you for taking the time to purchase The Would You Rather Book for Kids! We have spent countless hours putting together only the best and most interactive Would You Rather questions for the kids and the entire family to enjoy! You can expect to find 700+ different Would You Rather questions ranging from and even. These Would You Rather questions are guaranteed to make you think hard and have all kinds of fun while doing so.

The Would You Rather Book for Kids is very versatile! Use it on your own before bed, with friends at a get together, with family at the dinner table or camping with relatives; the possibilities with it are endless. Be creative and utilize it to its full potential!

Now, it's time to go over the instructions and how to play. The next chapter will cover every detail you need to know!

INSTRUCTIONS

Would You Rather questions have proven for many years to be one of the best ways to pass time with friends and family in a fun and interactive way. If you have never played before, here are some guidelines to follow in order to have the best experience possible!

1. Find 1 to as many people as you can to play with!

Although you could play alone, we suggest playing with at least 1 friend or more! This will add to the fun of the experience. If you happen to have more than one other person to play with, simply split your friends and yourself into 2 groups.

2. **Pick a team to start!**

When it comes to starting to read out the questions, the team that doesn't go first will read out the first question to the other team. This process will flip back and forth for each and every question in the book.

3. **The team being asked the question must choose one of the options!**

The team that gets the question read to them first must choose between one of the questions and give a reason for why they picked it

4. **Continue this process until one of the teams can't choose!**

The first team that can't decide on an option for one of

the questions loses. Of course, everybody wins in a question game, so have fun and see who can give the best answers!

Have fun and be sure to share this book and game with as many friends and family as possible!

FUNNY & SILLY QUESTIONS!

1. Would you rather meet a friendly dinosaur or meet a friendly dragon?

2. Would you rather wake up with wings or wake up with a tail?

3. Would you rather be in a food fight or just watch a food fight?

4. Would you rather kiss a frog or hug a snake?

5. Would you rather be able to spit out ice or spit out fire?

6. Would you rather be able to talk to animals or be able to hear animals talk?

7. Would you rather have a pet panda bear or a pet sloth?

8. Would you rather have green eyes or yellow eyes?

9. Would you rather have three eyes or two mouths?

10. Would you rather have a flying carpet or a car that can drive underwater?

11. Would you rather jump into a pool of chocolate pudding or a pool of strawberry ice cream?

12. Would you rather drink with your nose or toot with your mouth?

13. Would you rather be in your favorite video game or be in your favorite cartoon?

14. Would you rather make loud burps that are hard to ignore or burps that make no noise?

15. Would you rather have a unicorn of your own or be a unicorn?

16. Would you rather have a rabbit's ears or a rabbit's teeth?

17. Would you rather have to wear a clown wig or a clown nose for the rest of your life?

18. Would you rather meet a donkey that walks on two legs or a donkey that talks?

19. Would you rather have hair that smells like chocolate or hair that smells like Strawberry?

20. Would you rather have no eyebrows or have pink eyebrows?

21. Would you rather have milk run down your nose every time you laugh or have milk run out of your eyes every time you cried?

22. Would you rather have your leg stuck in the toilet bowl or have your hands stuck in the toilet bowl?

23. Would you rather lick milk like a cat or lick yourself like a cat?

24. Would you rather dance around the house in your underwear or dance around the neighborhood barefooted?

25. Would you rather be without a nose or be without ears?

26. Would you rather have to do jumping jacks every hour or have to do pushups every hour?

27. Would you rather not be able to taste anything or not be able to smell anything?

28. Would you rather have six fingers or have six toes?

29. Would you rather have gum stuck to the bottom of your shoe or tissue paper stuck to the bottom of your shoe?

30. Would you rather touch fire or spikes?

31. Would you rather have a stain on your outfit and not notice or a hole in your outfit and not notice?

32. Would you rather be pranked or be a well-known prankster?

33. Would you rather meet a friendly monster or a monster who's looking for friends?

34. Would you rather be bald or have hair that's almost touching the floor?

35. Would you rather have really long fingernails or really long toenails?

36. Would you rather be stuck in school for a year or get assignments every single day for a year?

37. Would you rather brush your teeth with ketchup or brush your teeth with hot sauce?

38. Would you rather have a really scary smile or have a really loud laugh?

39. Would you rather be able to read the minds of babies or be able to communicate with babies?

40. Would you rather eat a year's worth of pizza in one night or never eat pizza again?

41. Would you rather have embarrassing pictures of you posted online or sent to your crush?

42. Would you rather have a baby throw up on you or a baby toot on you?

43. Would you rather dance like a chicken in front of your friends or dance like a chicken on the internet?

44. Would you rather walk like a giraffe or walk like a frog?

45. Would you rather have a squeaky voice or a really loud voice?

46. Would you rather get into a fight with ducks or get chased by ducks?

47. Would you rather have a toy that walks or a toy that talks?

48. Would you rather find a cockroach hiding in your pizza or a cockroach hiding in your shoe?

49. Would you rather choke on your spit while talking or spit in someone's face while talking?

50. Would you rather be pranked with a fake rat or a fake bug?

51. Would you rather pee in a bucket or pee in a cup?

52. Would you rather have two tongues or no tongue?

53. Would you rather have a bird make a nest in your hair or a chicken lay eggs in your hair?

54. Would you rather have blue skin like an alien or really purple skin like barney?

55. Would you rather have multicolored hair or hair that tastes like candy?

56. Would you rather live in the sky permanently or live underwater permanently?

57. Would you rather be able to make your favorite food appear out of thin air or make your worst food disappear into thin air?

58. Would you rather be able to turn yourself into a butterfly or be able to turn yourself into an eagle?

59. Would you rather be able to climb walls like a spider or run as fast as a rodent?

60. Would you rather be able to talk to animals or be able to be an animal of your choice?

61. Would you rather look really old or look like a newborn baby again?

62. Would you rather eat a piece of gum from the street or give your already chewed gum to someone else?

63. Would you rather sleep beside a skunk or sleep beside a pig?

64. Would you rather eat only donuts for an entire week or never get to eat donuts for the rest of your life?

65. Would you rather wear a clown's costume or have your best friend wear a clown's costume?

66. Would you rather have an itch you can't scratch or an itch that refuses to go away?

67. Would you dip your face into a plate of vinegar or into a plate of blended garlic?

68. Would you rather live in a world full of zombies or a world full of aliens?

69. Would you rather go to a dance with someone who has bad breath or someone who has body odor?

70. Would you rather have your mom embarrass you at school or have your friend embarrass you at school?

71. Would you rather run for 10 minutes or walk for 1 hour?

72. Would you rather be the star player on a losing sports team at school or ride the bench on a sports team that always wins?

73. Would you rather sing with a crooked voice in front of your schoolmates or sing in a crooked voice in front of complete strangers?

74. Would you rather be stuck in a room with a clown that's not funny or with a clown that's quite annoying?

75. Would you rather your underwear were all pink or all your underwear had holes in them?

76. Would you rather wake up with your grandma's face or wake up with your grandpa's face?

77. Would you rather have nosy friends or noisy friends?

78. Would you rather be very unpopular or be super popular and be stalked by paparazzi all the time?

79. Would you rather only be able to listen to music from the 60's, or never be able to listen to music again?

80. Would you rather be stuck on an island alone or be stuck with someone who won't stop screaming?

81. Would you rather live in a cave alone or live in a cave with a friendly bear?

82. Would you rather be stuck with a crying baby for the weekend or with a baby that likes to drag your hair?

83. Would you rather have really large feet or feet so small you have to shop for shoes at the baby's department?

84. Would you rather kiss your Teddy bear before sleeping or whisper to it all through the night?

85. Would you rather sleep alone when it's raining heavily or creep into your sibling's room and snuggle up with them?

86. Would you rather run from a rabbit that talks or a rabbit that walks on two feet?

87. Would you rather have hair grow on your tongue or have hair grow in between your teeth?

88. Would you rather throw up on your crush or throw up on your best friend?

89. Would you rather sing loudly in the shower or sing loudly while on the toilet seat?

90. Would you rather drop your phone or drop your school lunch?

91. Would you rather spy on your neighbor or sneak into your neighbor's house while they're asleep?

92. Would you rather toot in an elevator or toot in class?

93. Would you rather wear pajamas to class or go to class in your underwear?

94. Would you rather do a prank phone call or send a prank text?

95. Would you rather eat food from the floor or eat food straight from the pot?

96. Would you rather swim in ice-cold water or swim in a pool of hot water?

97. Would you rather eat an entire cake on your own or eat 12 boxes of pizza on your own?

98. Would you rather roll down the stairs or hop down the stairs?

99. Would you rather have food spilled all over your favorite outfit or have a drink spilled all over your favorite outfit?

100.   Would you rather ride on the back of a lion or ride on the back of a tiger?

101.   Would you rather tickle your dad while he's sleeping or tickle your mom she sleeping?

102.   Would you rather have to ride an elephant or a camel to school every day?

103.   Would you rather have to drink everything from your ears or eat everything with your bellybutton?

104.   Would you rather have to eat two full lumps of sugar or eat one small pinch of salt?

105.   Would you rather sweat sticky lemonade or have your breath always smell like garlic?

106.   Would you rather forever have to eat with your feet or walk with your hands?

107.   Would you rather sound like a cow mooing every time you laughed or sound like a chicken every time your screamed?

108.   Would you rather have a single pair of eyes on the back of your head of one pair of eyes on each side of your head?

109.   Would you rather have a house that is built with jello or a car that is made with graham crackers and honey?

110.   Would you rather possess the ability to know what your classmates are thinking or be completely invisible?

111.   Would you rather eat however many teddy grahams or fish crackers that you wanted?

112.   Would you rather have a pie smashed onto your face or be sprayed all over your body with silly string?

113.   Would you rather have 10 fingers on each of your hands or 10 toes on each foot?

114.   Would you rather name your own island or be able to name your own sports team?

115.   Would you rather have to brush your teeth with baking soda or dish soap?

116.   Would you rather look at everything that's far away by using binoculars or look at tiny things close up with a microscope

117.   Would you rather swim in a pool of chocolate or play on a field of milky way bars?

118.   Would you rather lay in bed with your favorite stuffed animal or your favorite blanket?

119.   Would you rather teleport into another country or into another world?

120.   Would you rather live with your parents or with your grandparents?

121.   Would you rather be unable to open any closed doors or not be able to close any open doors?

122.   Would you rather have tiny feet and huge hands or huge feet and tiny hands?

123.   Would you rather be able to design an imaginary creation just by drawing it or make something that is real disappear by erasing it?

124.   Would you rather be a superhero or a sidekick?

125.   Would you rather run as fast as a turtle but be able to fly or run as fast as a cheetah but not be able to fly?

126.   Would you rather go to bed with a friend in a tree house or in sleeping bags?

127.   Would you rather have a robot that is your friend, or that is your servant?

128.   Would you rather live on a farm on live in a big city?

129.   Would you rather be allowed to wear any type of clothing that you want to school or have to wear school uniforms?

130.   Would you rather put a hotdog in a hamburger bun or a hamburger in a hotdog bun?

131. Would you rather constantly have to sneeze but it never comes out or have hiccups that last for four hours per day?

132. Would you rather have to use your weak hand to eat or to write?

133. Would you rather go back in time one year to talk to your past self or go into the future one year to talk to future self?

134. Would you rather have to shave all of your hair or lose all of your teeth?

135. Would you rather have to pay for everything with pennies or 100 dollar bills for the rest of your life?

136. Would you rather eat wet cat food or dog treats after breakfast, lunch, and dinner?

137. Would you rather have a camera as your eyes or a sound recorder as your ears?

138.   Would you rather find out that you are an adopted child or discover that all of your siblings are adopted?

139.   Would you rather never know what you look like or never know what any of your family looks like?

140.   Would you rather have to drink all of your beverages from a huge bucket or a baby bottle?

141.   Would you rather wear the same clothes to school every day or have your parents pick out a new outfit for you every day?

142.   Would you rather have teeth that are super crooked or teeth that are as yellow as a banana?

143.   Would you rather have short and stubby legs or long and lanky arms?

144.   Would you rather sit or stand for the rest of your life if you could only choose one?

145.   Would you rather float every time you tried to jump or jump every time you tried to walk?

146.   Would you rather have to fight 100 pigeon sized zebras or one zebra sized pigeon?

147.   Would you rather have two huge, yellow front teeth like a beaver or two pinching teeth like a beetle?

148.   Would you rather see colors that no one else could see or smell smells that no one else could?

149.   Would you rather visit a good amusement park once every month or go to the best amusement park in the world once every year?

150.   Would you rather have a secret switch that would make your brothers and sisters quiet or have a secret switch that could make your mom and dad quiet?

151.   Would you rather be able to live as long as you wanted or be the strongest superhero in the whole world?

152.   Would you rather possess the power to never get sick for the entirety of your life or to never get injured?

153.   Would you rather struggle with an itch that you could never reach or only be able to use one sheet of toilet paper the entire day?

154.   Would you rather have to run in a potato sack bag or travel everywhere in a wheelchair?

155.   Would you rather have a food fight or a water balloon fight with your family?

156.   Would you rather blow out 50 butterflies every time you sneeze or cough out a mouse every time you wheeze?

157.   Would you rather be forced to say everything that was on your mind or to never speak unless someone spoke to you?

HARDEST QUESTIONS!

1. Would you rather have to live the rest of your life without a phone or a television?

2. Would you rather have hardly any money but lots of friends or be rich and have no friends?

3. Would you rather sleep 20 hours per day or two hours per day for the rest of your life?

4. Would you rather live without heating in the winter or air conditioning in the summer?

5. Would you rather use your hands as your feet or your feet as your hands?

6. Would you rather be the speediest person in the world or be able to jump the highest?

7. Would you rather live way down in the sea or fly high in the sky for the rest of your life?

8. Would you rather be the most famous actor or famous singer?

9. Would you rather have hair so long that it touched the ground or have no hair at all for the rest of your life?

10. Would you rather possess the ability to smell like a hound dog or have the eyesight of an eagle?

11. Would you rather take one single one-month long vacation or four one-week long vacations every year?

12. Would you rather if your toes were your fingers or your fingers be your toes?

13. Would you rather turn into a dog or a cat for the rest of your life?

14. Would you rather time travel 100 years back in history or 100 years into the future?

15. Would you rather eat pizza each and every breakfast or cereal and milk for every dinner?

16. Would you rather live to be 100 years old or 1000 years old?

17. Would you rather not ever have to go to school or never have to do chores for the rest of your life?

18. Would you rather possess the face of a 10 year old and the body of a 50 year old or the face of a 50 year old and the body of a 10 year old?

19. Would you rather always need to shout whenever you speak or always have to whisper?

20. Would you rather live one single life that lasted 1000 years or 10 different lives that each lasted 100?

21. Would you rather have 10 siblings or only one sibling?

22. Would you rather have to sleep in the wilderness or in a sleeping bag for the rest of your life?

23. Would you rather be the President of the United States or just an average person?

24. Would you rather have to share your house with two lions or with 1000 honeybees?

25. Would you rather forever be the youngest sibling or forever be the oldest sibling?

26. Would you rather not have to go to school but have 12 hours of homework or go to school for 12 hours but not have any homework?

27. Would you rather it snow every single day or rain every single day?

28. Would you rather be the best artist in the world or the best sports player in the world?

29. Would you rather have to read at least one book every week or never read a book again?

30. Would you rather be able to travel anywhere in outer space or straight into the middle of the earth?

31. Would you rather have a single best friend who you could trust all the time or 10 good friends who you could trust only sometimes?

32. Would you rather only be able to watch movies in the movie theater or in your home for the rest of your life?

33. Would you rather only be able to watch TV shows or movies for the rest of your life?

34. Would you rather only be able to drink apple juice or milk for every meal of the day?

35. Would you rather have a tiny freckle right in the middle of your forehead or one huge freckle on your arm?

36. Would you rather stay young for as long as you live or be an adult as soon as you were born?

37. Would you rather drive in a police car or in a fire truck?

38. Would you rather earn 1,000 dollars per day for your whole entire life or have the chance to win 100 million dollars?

39. Would you rather have a personal interview with your favorite actor or be in a movie with them?

40. Would you rather take care of other people's kids or other people's dogs?

41. Would you rather be able to eat ice-cream for every meal or have a famous ice-cream bar named after you?

42. Would you rather have to ride a train to get everywhere or always have to take an airplane?

43. Would you rather be the tallest person in the world or the shortest person in the world?

44. Would you rather be extremely healthy but never eat desserts or be extremely unhealthy but be able to eat any food that you want?

45. Would you rather make 1,000 dollars a day but never see your family or make 10 dollars a day and always be able to see your family?

46. Would you rather turn into your mom or your dad for one day if you could only choose one?

47. Would you rather be able to understand animals but they not be able to understand you or not be able to understand animals but they understand you?

48. Would you rather always see the world in black and white or always see the world in color but with stripes?

49. Would you rather always be dressed up in your fanciest clothes or always be dressed up in your dirtiest clothes?

50. Would you rather never know what time it is or never know what day it is?

51. Would you rather only be able to celebrate Halloween or only be able to celebrate your birthday?

52. Would you rather buy 100 one dollar toys or buy one 100 dollar toy?

53. Would you rather buy 100 one dollar toys or buy one 100 dollar toy?

54. Would you rather be able to play any new video game that comes out or be able to get the latest new phone when it comes out?

55. Would you rather it be necessary to use a bike or use a scooter to get around everywhere?

56. Would you rather only live to be 50 years old but be rich or live to 100 years old but be poor.

57. Would you rather be the world's most famous singer or the most famous dancer?

58. Would you rather have a nose the size of Pinocchio's or ears as large as Dumbo's?

59. Would you rather have to eat a diet that was only plants or eat a diet that was only meat?

60. Would you rather buy your own amusement park like Disney or buy your own private island?

61. Would you rather have water that tastes like your favorite drink or vegetables that taste like your favorite dessert?

62. Would you rather be able to skip all of your dentist appointments or all of your doctor's appointments?

63. Would you rather win a lottery ticket worth 100,000 dollars or have your friend win a lottery ticket worth 1,000,000 dollars?

64. Would you rather only be able to see out of one eye or only be able to hear out of one ear?

65. Would you rather never be able to see your grandparents again or never be able to see your best friends again?

66. Would you rather be able to stay up as long as you wanted or sleep in as long as you wanted?

67. Would you rather eat homemade meals or fast food for every single meal as long as you lived?

68. Would you rather be the best player on a winning team or the worst player on a losing team?

69. Would you rather be required to use a spoon or a fork every time you eat if you could only choose one?

70. Would you rather only be able to watch one TV show or have to watch all of your TV show's in black and white?

71. Would you rather read an excellent book or watch a great movie?

72. Would you rather be all alone in the desert or in the jungle?

73. Would you rather spoil a movie for a friend that they haven't watched or have a friend spoil a movie that you haven't watched?

74. Would you rather be the center of attention or stand in the corner at a party?

75. Would you rather be able to speak to any animal or know every language in the world?

GROSS QUESTIONS!

1. Would you rather have to eat a chili flavored wasp or a sugar coated cricket?

2. Would you rather win a hot dog eating contest or a cheeseburger eating contest?

3. Would you rather have to sneeze every 10 minutes or burp every 10 minutes?

4. Would you rather swim with the dolphins or fly with the birds?

5. Would you rather forever have a string of snot hanging out of your nostril or always sneeze out a booger?

6. Would you rather have one eye in the middle of your head or two noses?

7. Would you rather sleep with snails or sleep with spiders?

8. Would you rather need to use a litter box to use the bathroom or use the bathroom outdoors?

9. Would you rather have to take a bath drenched in honey or a shower sprayed with sticky syrup?

10. Would you rather never be able to brush your teeth again or never be able to take a shower again?

11. Would you rather have 100 cockroaches in your room or have to eat one cockroach?

12. Would you rather pet a slimy eel or have to pet a prickly porcupine?

13. Would you rather sweat every single time you went outside or only take a shower once per month?

14. Would you rather have hair covering your entire body or have feathers covering your body?

15. Would you rather drink water that had soap within it or drink water that had mud within it?

16. Would you rather munch on a grape that had mold on it or drink water that had muck within it?

17. Would you rather step in pee in the bathroom or have to sit down on a disgusting toilet?

18. Would you rather have to smell your entire family's underwear every morning or their socks every afternoon?

19. Would you rather have booger flavored ice cream or ice cream flavored boogers?

20. Would you rather have gum stuck in your hair or inside of both of your shoes?

21. Would you rather have a huge piece of green salad stuck in your teeth or a booger stuck in your nostril?

22. Would you rather not wash your armpits or not rinse your hands for an entire week?

23. Would you rather walk barefoot through horse manure or through poison ivy?

24. Would you rather have a baby puke on you or sneeze on you?

25. Would you rather not take a bath for one month or not change your clothes for one month?

26. Would you rather pick someone else's earwax or clip someone else's disgusting toenails?

27. Would you rather be a unicorn or a pegasus?

28. Would you rather come across a rat in your box of cereal or in your carton of milk?

29. Would you rather stink like rotten meat every time you run or every time you go swimming?

30. Would you rather have to smell your friend's feet or have your friend smell your feet?

31. Would you rather cough candy or cough lemonade every?

32. Would you rather wear used socks and underwear or a used toothbrush?

33. Would you rather throw up or dance super loudly in front of your favorite singer?

34. Would you rather be fully covered in mud or completely covered in sticky honey?

35. Would you rather have to eat the diet of a shark or the diet of pig for every meal of the day?

36. Would you rather have fingernails or toenails that are covered in mud and dirt?

37. Would you rather have to wear a stinky pair of shoes or socks to school every day?

38. Would you rather be unable to wash any of your shirts or any of your shorts for an entire year?

39. Would you rather have earwax in your nostrils or boogers in your ears?

40. Would you rather be confined in the saliva or the nose of a giant?

41. Would you rather have to lick your own sweaty armpit or bite off your own dirty fingernail?

42. Would you rather have to drink spoiled milk or eat a rotten banana?

43. Would you rather forever eat your least favorite food or someone else's boogers once at every meal?

44. Would you rather have to see poison ivy or a small colony of fire ants?

45. Would you rather look amazing but smell as bad as a skunk or look bad but smell amazing?

46. Would you rather have a 30 foot anaconda or a stinky elephant as your school mascot?

47. Would you rather burp uncontrollably for one hour after breakfast or toot continuously for 30 minutes after dinner?

48. Would you rather have wings but you can't fly or have gills but you can't swim underwater?

49. Would you rather have to use leaves for your toilet paper or mayonnaise for your soap?

50. Would you rather have to eat frog's legs or pig's feet for every meal the rest of your life?

51. Would you rather have to toot 10 times every hour or 1 time every minute?

52. **Would you rather have to eat a super spicy food or the most bitter food in the entire world?**

53. **Would you rather have a hand twice as big or half as small?**

54. **Would you rather eat a raw potato or a whole lime?**

55. **Would you rather never have to shower again or never have to clip your toenails?**

56. **Would you rather only be able to crawl on all fours or only be able to walk backwards?**

WEIRD QUESTIONS!

1. Would you rather have to wear a clown mask or a superhero mask everyday for the rest of your life?

2. Would you rather have ears that turned green every time you got angry or a nose that turned black every time you smile?

3. Would you rather have to wear a pair of shoes that was one size too large or one size too little?

4. Would you rather consume an entire serving of pasta that was completely overcooked or would you rather be required to eat an entire serving of dry rice?

5. Would you rather have eyeballs made out of jello or a nose made out of fruit loops?

6. Would you rather have plants grow 10 times larger than normal or have animals shrink 10 times smaller than they were before?

7. Would you rather be as thin as a sheet or paper or as fat as a giant hot air balloon.

8. Would you rather your entire house be as bouncy as a trampoline or sink in like quicksand?

9. Would you rather have a babysitter who doesn't play with you or one who doesn't know how to cook very well?

10. Would you rather be able to push things away from you or pull them towards you just by looking at them?

11. Would you rather be required to say hello to every person you saw or never say hello to anybody?

12. Would you rather be given a bad haircut every time or always have horrible breath?

13. Would you rather be able to eat as much as you want without getting sick or get as much sleep as you want?

14. Would you rather begin your life in the past or the future if you could be born again?

15. Would you rather consume a sandwich with no bread or a cheeseburger with no meat?

16. Would you rather grow antenna's like a bug or grow a fluffy tail like a rabbit?

HOLIDAY QUESTIONS!

1. Would you rather have to sing Holiday songs in a church choir or sing them at your school?

2. Would you rather have to shovel snow every day during break or not have any snow at all?

3. Would you rather be required to have the bristles of a tree as your hair or tree pine cones as your ears?

4. Would you rather have to write a 10 page essay about summer or do 10 pages of math over your Holiday break?

5. Would you rather have your room redecorated however you want or ten toys of your choice (can be any price)?

6. Would you rather eat each of the cookies or drink all of the milk during Holidays?

7. Would you rather get coal in your stocking or get no gifts at all?

8. Would you rather have to write down all of the gifts that children wanted or wrap all of the gifts during your birthday?

9. Would you rather live in a house shaped like a circle or a house shaped like a triangle?

10. Would you rather have to wear lights around your body or have jingle bells attached around your waist?

11. Would you rather have chocolate milk be the only drink that you can have or gingerbread muffins be the only treat that you eat?

12. Would you rather have to drink gravy instead of water or eat the entire turkey?

13. Would you rather show up to school wearing a Halloween outfit or a Batman outfit?

14. Would you rather play in one foot of snow or play when there is no snow at all?

15. Would you rather wander off somewhere in a tree farm or have snowballs thrown at you?

16. Would you rather give one gift to someone who doesn't have any gifts or keep 10 gifts for yourself?

17. Would you rather get 10 pieces of candy or 10 small toys in your Halloween stocking?

18. Would you rather get coal in your stocking or have only one Birthday gift?

19. Would you rather be given a birthday gift that is fun to play with or that serves a purpose?

20. Would you rather have a winter break that is as long as summer break or a summer break that is as short as winter break?

21. Would you rather help make an excellent Thanksgiving meal or help decorate the Turkey tray?

22. Would you rather have two candy canes or one treat that you could choose every day?

23. Would you rather put up super hero themed Halloween decorations or Disney themed decorations?

24. Would you rather never eat cheese again or never drink anything sweet again during the holidays?

25. Would you rather get the best gift ever but have to give it away or get an okay gift but keep it?

26. For your holidays, would you rather have an amazing tree house with slides and three rooms or an amazing entertainment system with a huge TV and every game console?

27. Would you rather play outdoors or indoors during your birthday?

28. Would you rather be forced to wear a red nose to school or dress up as Justin Bieber for one week?

29. Would you rather be best friends with your math teacher during holidays or your English teacher?

30. Would you rather never be able to eat treats again or never celebrate Halloween again?

31. Would you rather talk like you're singing a melody or sing like you're talking during your birthday?

32. Would you rather have five people to celebrate Halloween with or 500 people?

33. Would you rather instantly become a grown up or stay the age you are now for another two years?

34. Would you rather meet your favorite celebrity or be on a TV show during the holidays?

35. Would you rather be the only kid in the entire world who didn't get a holiday present or the only kid who did get one?

36. Would you rather get stuck in a chimney or be yourself but have to wear a different sweater every day of the year?

37. Would you rather play in a snowball fight or build a snowman if you could only choose one?

38. Would you rather peak at your presents before opening them or get one extra present?

39. Would you rather get socks or underwear from your grandparents on Thanksgiving?

40. Would you rather see your dad dance on your birthday or have the most presents you've ever had?

41. Would you rather have to wear a beard for your whole entire life or have the longest hair in the world?

42. Would you rather get 1,000 dollars or 10 great gifts for your birthday?

43. Would you rather have the chance to design a new toy or create a new TV show during your holidays?

44. Would you rather drink hot chocolate or apple cider for all of Thanksgiving?

45. Would you rather have a frigid Birthday with lots of snow or a warm Birthday with no snow?

46. Would you rather be a penguin or a polar bear in Antarctica?

47. Would you rather stick your hand in a freezing bucket of water or have 100 snowballs dumped straight on your head?

48. Would you rather dance in front of 1000 people or sing in front of 1000 people on your birthday?

49. Would you rather watch Halloween movies all day or go Halloween shopping all day?

50. Would you rather sleep through all of thanksgiving Day or not get any good presents on your birthday?

51. Would you rather have 10 presents wrapped in huge boxes or 10 presents wrapped in small boxes?

52. Would you rather tie a bow around 100 gifts or wrap up 100 gifts?

53. Would you rather go back to the past to your favorite thanksgiving Day or travel into the future to a random thanksgiving Day?

54. Would you rather trade all of your birthday gifts with your best friend or a random person?

55. Would you rather know exactly what presents you're getting one month before your birthday or have to wait one week after to open up all of your gifts?

56. Would you rather spend every Thanksgiving with good friends and family but not have any friends or family?

RANDOM QUESTIONS!

1. Would you rather have an aunt that pulls your cheeks a lot or an aunt that pats your head a lot?

2. Would you rather forget to take your toothbrush for a sleepover or forget to take your towel for a sleepover?

3. Would you rather scream while watching a scary movie or pee in your pants while watching a scary movie?

4. Would you rather have a nose as long as Pinocchio's or no nose at all?

5. Would you rather eat your fingernails or eat your toenails?

6. **Would you rather forget the way to school or forget the way to your class?**

7. **Would you rather have something stuck in your teeth and not know or have something dangling out of your nose and not know?**

8. **Would you rather have your diary read out in public or eaten by your dog?**

9. **Would you rather wake up beside a cartoon character or beside someone you've never seen before?**

10. **Would you rather have the entire school know who you're crushing on or never get to see your crush again?**

11. **Would you rather eat a snail or have a snail as a pet?**

12. **Would you rather fall asleep in class or fall asleep on the bus?**

13. Would you rather eat food out of the trashcan or not get any food to eat for an entire weekend?

14. Would you rather walk into the wrong house on your way back from school or walk into the wrong class at school?

15. Would you rather trip and fall while running away from someone or trip and fall while running towards someone?

16. Would you rather have a massive zit or a zit that won't go away?

17. Would you rather close your eyes tight when a scary scene in a movie came on or run out of the room when a scary scene in a movie came on?

18. Would you rather have soda come out of your nose or come back out of your mouth?

19. Would you rather sit on something really wet or sit on something really cold?

20. Would you rather see a funny video of your parents online or see a funny video of a close friend online?

21. Would you rather be licked all over by a stray dog or be followed all around by a stray dog?

22. Would you rather swim in a pool that your friend peed in or pee in a pool?

23. Would you rather become a dolphin or have a best friend who's a dolphin?

24. Would you rather stroke a friendly lion that's awake or stroke an unfriendly lion while it's asleep?

25. Would you rather walk around with soap in your hair or with an unkempt hair?

26. Would you rather wear ugly shoes or shoes that are much bigger than your feet?

27. Would you rather lick your foot or lick your friend's foot?

28. Would you rather have a really fat tummy or a tummy that makes rumbling noises a lot?

29. Would you rather stain your mouth with chicken sauce and not know or stain your hands with chicken sauce and not have anything to clean it with?

30. Would you rather roll off your bed or roll onto your teddy bear?

31. Would you rather have smelly hair or badly trimmed hair?

32. Would you rather sound like an old person or look like an old person?

33. Would you rather drop your new phone down to the toilet or drop your charm bracelet down the sink?

34. **Would you rather get a brain freeze every time you drank something cold or stop drinking anything cold altogether?**

35. **Would you rather a tooth fairy ran off with your tooth and left nothing or left a golden tooth?**

36. **Would you rather scratch your butt in public or scratch your armpit in public?**

37. **Would you rather wear dirty clothes for a week of wear the same outfit every day for a week?**

38. **Would you rather forget your lines during a class presentation or during a debate in front of the entire school?**

39. **Would you rather produce toots that smell good or toots that have no smell at all?**

40. **Would you rather eat fish that's half done or fish that's half burnt?**

41. Would you rather roll in mud or have mud splashed all over you?

42. Would you rather be an Internet sensation from doing something embarrassing or from doing something nerdy?

43. Would you rather slip on a banana peel or slip while trying to avoid a banana peel?

44. Would you rather dig through a dumpster or fall into a dumpster?

45. Would you rather have all your teeth fall out or have only two teeth?

46. Would you rather have claws as hands or have a hook as a hand?

47. Would you rather have one leg shorter than the other or two really short legs?

48. Would you rather have the zip of your jeans cut or the button on your jeans fall off?

49. Would you rather wear wet underwear or dirty underwear?

50. Would you rather pop a balloon with something sharp or blow a balloon till it pops?

51. Would you rather share your bed with someone who snores or someone who talks in their sleep?

52. Would you rather be in a Disney animation or in a Disney movie?

53. Would you rather have a discussion with a robot from your planet or an alien from a foreign planet?

54. Would you rather have feet that were wheels or have hands that were boxing gloves?

55. Would you rather have eyebrows that never stopped growing or have no eyebrows at all?

56. Would you rather have robots, or space aliens invade our planet and take over the world?

57. Would you rather wash all of your clothes or all of your dishes with your tongue?

58. Would you rather have venomous fangs like a snake for teeth or sharp talons like an eagle as fingers?

59. Would you rather have to wrestle a grizzly bear or a lion?

60. Would you rather wear super fancy shoes or casual slippers everywhere you went?

61. Would you rather have to wear your grandfather's clothes or have your grandfather's hair style?

62. Would you rather go all the way back in time when the dinosaurs lived or when the Woolly Mammoth's lived?

63. Would you rather wake up in the morning and be in outer space or in another country?

64. Would you rather shrink a tiny bit every time you sneezed or grow a tiny bit taller every time you coughed?

65. Would you rather drink vegetable flavored juice or eat juice flavored vegetables?

66. Would you rather rule over the entire world but never be satisfied or never rule over the world but always be joyful?

67. Would you rather get stuck in an elevator with five monkeys or with 20 people?

68. Would you rather be able to control when it rains or when it snows?

69. Would you rather have extremely long hair coming out of your ears or out of your nostrils?

70. Would you rather have to dye your hair ten different colors or cut all of your hair off?

71. Would you rather teleport straight into a video game or straight into your favorite TV show?

72. Would you rather laugh every time someone said something serious or cry every time someone said something funny?

73. Would you rather transform into a puppy every time you eat something or turn into a cat every time you drink something?

74. Would you rather turn the color of whatever you drink or whatever you eat every single time?

75. Would you rather wear mismatched socks and shoes or mismatched earrings to school every day?

76. Would you rather wear flip flops in the frigid snow or wear four layers of clothing when it is super hot?

77. Would you rather your head be two times as large as a normal head or have a head that is half the size of a normal head?

78. Would you rather be the cow in all of the Chick-fil-A commercials or the king in all of the burger king commercials?

79. Would you rather have a snout nose like a pig or huge ears like an elephant

80. Would you rather possess the ability to smell sounds or be able to hear smells?

81. Would you rather be able to turn the moon into creamy cheese or your house into delicious candy?

82. Would you rather be able to find out what your parent's think or what your teacher's think?

83. Would you rather have an unlimited amount of treats or an endless amount of happiness?

84. Would you rather have Cheeto grime all over your fingers or have sweaty feet all the time?

85. Would you rather have an oversized pet gerbil the size of a horse or a tiny horse the size of a gerbil?

86. Would you rather have to take a freezing cold shower or a super hot shower every morning?

87. Would you rather swim in a swimming pool with 10 goats or with 100 mice?

88. Would you rather have to close your eyes when you go to the movies or when you go to a water park?

89. Would you rather be isolated on an island with your favorite singer or with your favorite animal?

90. Would you rather be in jail for five years or in a hospital for 10 years?

91. Would you rather begin your life with an alien family in outer space or with a family of giraffes?

92. Would you rather be the most popular animal in the entire world or a regular person who was not popular?

93. Would you rather be the smartest person in the world, but you couldn't speak or an average person but you could speak?

94. Would you rather eat your favorite meal or eat a meal you've never had before?

95. Would you rather be popular among your classmates or be popular among your teachers?

96. Would you rather be in a house filled with marshmallows or a house filled with candy?

97. Would you rather be given apples to eat or be given vegetables to eat?

98. Would you rather have bright pink hair or bright brown hair?

99. Would you rather it was winter all the time or that it was summer all the time?

100. Would you rather wear trendy sneakers or wear cute shoes?

101. Would you rather clean up your bathroom or clean up your bedroom?

102. Would you rather get a huge bowl of punch or get a huge bowl of ice-cream?

103. Would you rather be a doctor or a teacher?

104. Would you rather get a toy boat or go see a real life ship?

105. Would you rather have your friends come over or go outside and play with your friends?

106. Would you rather go for a stroll or drive around with dad in his car?

107.   Would you rather have only white clothes or only multicolored clothes?

108.   Would you rather go camping or go fishing?

109.   Would you rather have your mom stay at home all day or go with mom to work?

110.   Would you rather take the stairs or take the elevator?

111.   Would you rather have pizza or have a hotdog?

112.   Would you rather eat your chips with ketchup or eat your chips with mustard?

113.   Would you rather go to school with your friend on the public bus or with mom and dad?

114.   Would you rather do hand-painting or paint with a brush?

115.   Would you rather go swimming or relax beside the pool?

116.   Would you rather get a cat or get a dog?

117.   Would you rather pet a giraffe or pet a hippopotamus?

118.   Would you rather watch people ice-skate or go ice-skating?

119.   Would you rather be really huge or be really strong?

120.   Would you rather go to bed early or wake up early?

121.   Would you rather cuddle a big teddy or cuddle with mom?

122.   Would you rather be a ninja or be a spy?

123.   Would you rather meet a fairy or meet a goddess?

124.   Would you rather go to a birthday party or plan a birthday party?

125.   Would you rather have a big room or a big backyard?

126.   Would you rather live with grandma or live with your cousins?

127.   Would you rather put up Thanksgiving decorations or help with the cooking?

128.   Would you rather go to a boarding school or go to a day school?

129.   Would you rather be homeschooled or go to a regular school?

130.   Would you rather be in a dance class or be in the choir?

131.   Would you rather watch a debate or be in the debate club?

132.   Would you rather shower with cold water or with hot water?

133.   Would you rather lose your favorite blanket or your favorite Teddy bear?

134.   Would you rather watch cartoons or dress up as cartoon characters?

135.   Would you rather be the last born or have a baby sister?

136.   Would you rather listen to an audiobook or read a hardcover book?

137.   Would you rather find a pony on your own or be surprised with a pony?

138.   Would you rather have all the drinks you could ever want or all the junk food you could ever want?

139.   Would you rather go to summer school or summer camp?

140.   Would you rather go to a tea party or a costume party?

141.   Would you rather get a trick or a treat?

142.   Would you rather play on the slides or on the trampoline?

143.   Would you rather get good grades or be really good at a sport?

144.   Would you rather help set the table for dinner or help clear the table after dinner?

145.   Would you rather only eat candy for the rest of your life or never eat candy again?

146. Would you rather go to the moon or go to the bottom of the ocean?

147. Would you rather go to a new school or move to a new house?

148. Would you rather build a snowman or build a sand castle?

149. Would you rather have a robot friend or a robot that can do anything you ask?

150. Would you rather be Spiderman's sidekick or Superman's sidekick?

151. Would you rather crawl around all the time or hop around all the time?

152. Would you rather drink hot chocolate or chocolate milk?

153. Would you rather travel by road or travel by air?

154.   Would you rather find a turtle in your swimming pool or find a goose in your swimming pool?

155.   Would you rather go to the library or have a library in your house?

156.   Would you rather help mom with the laundry or do the laundry all on your own?

157.   Would you rather be unable to celebrate Halloween or be unable to celebrate your birthday?

158.   Would you rather eat something roasted or eat something fried?

159.   Would you rather meet an alien or meet a god?

160.   Would you rather have a litter of kittens delivered to you or a litter of puppies?

161.   Would you rather visit a zoo or visit a jungle?

162.   During a game of hide and seek, would you rather hide under your bird or inside your closet?

163.   Would you rather have a babysitter who's really old or a babysitter who's really young?

164.   Would you rather play games on a phone or play a board game?

165.   Would you rather never have to brush your teeth again or never have to shower again?

166.   Would you rather see a shooting star or see a rainbow?

167.   Would you rather live in a really noisy neighborhood or live in a really quiet neighborhood?

168. Would you rather raise chickens or raise cows?

169. Would you rather live in a tree house or on a houseboat?

170. Would you rather be cold at night or be hot at night?

171. Would you rather sleep in a tent or sleep right underneath the stars?

172. Would you rather lose your favorite toy or lose all your savings?

173. Would you rather forget your friend's birthday or have your friend forget your birthday?

174. Would you rather wash dirty clothes or fold all the clothes?

175. Would you rather be much taller or much shorter?

176.   Would you rather live in a house with no power or a house with no running water?

177.   Would you rather go jogging or go running?

178.   Would you rather have milkshakes or have a smoothie?

179.   Would you rather forget how to read or forget how to write?

180.   Would you rather meet your ancestors or meet your great grandchildren?

181.   Would you rather wear any clothing of your choice to school or wear a school uniform?

182.   Would you rather eat oatmeal or eat cereal?

183.   Would you rather wear SpongeBob pajamas or Dora the Explorer pajamas?

184.   Would you rather eat homemade food or eat at a fast food?

185.   Would you rather sleep in your bed or sleep with your parents?

186.   Would you rather be able to draw or watch someone else draw?

187.   Would you rather be able to sew or be able to knit?

188.   Would you rather watch TV in bed alone or watch TV on the couch with your family?

189.   Would you rather know how to speak French fluently or speak Spanish fluently?

190.   Would you rather dance in front of your family members or dance before your friends?

191.   Would you rather have a nanny that makes terrible meals or a nanny that's boring?

192.   Would you rather be known as a genius or be known for being funny?

193.   Would you rather win a cash prize or win an item?

194.   Would you rather have a wall poster of your favorite hero or a picture of your favorite hero?

195.   Would you rather make new friends at a party or stick with your old friends at a party?

196.   Would you rather eat on the living room couch or eat in your bed?

197.   Would you rather have a jacuzzi or a pool?

198.   Would you rather eat bread with butter or with jam?

199. **Would you rather watch a funny YouTube video online or watch a cartoon on TV?**

200. **Would you rather get cotton candy or get ice-cream at a park?**

201. **Would you rather have only one close friend or lots of friends you're not too close to?**

202. **Would you rather eat something really hot or eat something really cold?**

203. **Would you rather have a lot of superpowers for one week or just one superpower for a month?**

204. **Would you rather have a sore throat or a cough?**

205. **Would you rather have a twin or be an only child?**

206.   Would you rather go watch a circus show or be a part of a circus show?

207.   Would you rather climb a tree live in a tree?

208.   Would you rather share your bed with someone who snores a lot or one who toots a lot?

209.   Would you rather be famous for something bad or be amazing at something and no one knows?

210.   Would you rather grow up into an adult overnight or stay young forever?

211.   Would you rather be famous but ugly or be unknown and really attractive?

212.   Would you rather meet your favorite celebrity or meet the president?

213.   Would you rather feed a horse or brush a horse?

214.   Would you rather your hands got dirty all the time or your feet got dirty all the time?

215.   Would you rather meet your favorite band or get five concert tickets for free?

216.   Would you rather get presents you don't like on your birthday or get no presents at all?

217.   Would you rather be bald or have really long hair?

218.   Would you rather be hungry all the time or be thirsty all the time?

219.   Would you rather take out the garbage or wash the garbage can?

220.   Would you rather always be an hour later to everywhere you go or an hour early to everywhere you go?

221.   Would you rather have all your shirts be oversized or be really tight?

222.   Would you rather have no friends or be surrounded by annoying people?

223.   Would you rather be in a room that's really dark but warm or a room that's really bright but cold?

224.   Would you rather have a friend who's super smart and proud or a friend who's unintelligent and humble?

225.   Would you rather be feared by all or be liked by all?

226.   Would you rather eat something that's peppery or eat something that's spicy?

227.   Would you rather have large feet or large hands?

228. Would you rather be unable to use Google or be unable to use social media apps?

229. Would you rather lose all your baby pictures or lose all the pictures from your last birthday?

230. Would you rather never have to go to bed again or never have to wake up early?

231. Would you rather get a free boat cruise or a free plane ticket?

232. Would you rather be able to read really fast or to understand what you read really fast?

233. Would you rather use glasses or get contact lenses?

234. Would you rather meet an Easter bunny or find lots of Easter eggs?

235. Would you rather get lots of hugs or lots of cuddles?

236.   Would you rather face your fears or forget you have fears?

237.   Would you rather have to dance every time you heard a song or sing every time you heard a song?

238.   Would you rather snitch on your best friend about something they did or get into trouble with your parents over something you didn't?

239.   Would you rather find your favorite socks that went missing or get brand new socks?

240.   Would you rather suck on an orange or drink orange juice?

241.   Would you rather go to a clothing store or go to a toy store?

242.   Would you rather have to stay up all night or sleep all day?

243. Would you rather be a superhero or a magic wizard?

244. Would you rather be the author of a best-selling a book or star in a movie?

245. Would you rather have a snowball fight or a water balloon fight?

246. Would you rather never have homework again or be paid to do your homework?

247. Would you rather eat a whole onion or eat a whole can of sardines?

248. Would you rather be able to breathe underwater or be able to run on top of water?

249. Would you rather have the ability to fly or have the ability to read minds?

250.　　Would you rather play inside or play outside?

251.　　Would you rather be really cold or be really hot?

252.　　Would you rather be able to smell only bad-smelling things or never be able to smell again?

253.　　Would you rather eat cake or eat ice cream?

254.　　Would you rather have 3 arms or have only 1 leg?

255.　　Would you rather have a pet rat or a pet spider?

256.　　Would you rather be on a small boat or be on a large ship?

257. Would you rather be stranded on a desert island or be stranded in the forest?

258. Would you rather have the talent to play any musical instrument that there is or have the talent to speak every language there is?

259. Would you rather go fishing or go hiking?

260. Would you rather have all the food you ever wanted or have all the toys you ever wanted?

261. Would you rather have super speed or super strength?

262. Would you rather be given $10 every day for the rest of your life or be given $$1,000 only once?

263. Would you rather swim indoors or outdoors?

264.   Would you rather stay up really late or wake up really early?

265.   Would you rather never have homework again or never take a test again?

266.   Would you rather live where you are forever or move to another country?

267.   Would you rather brush your teeth using two-month-old milk or a bar of soap?

268.   Would you rather have your own robot or a jetpack?

269.   Would you rather own an elephant-sized mouse or a mouse-sized elephant?

270.   Would you rather eat chicken-flavored cookies or onion-flavored ice cream?

271.   Would you rather ride own a personal jet or your own helicopter?

272.   Would you rather be a bird or a fish?

273.   Would you rather be stung by a bee once or be bitten by a mosquito 10 times?

274.   Would you rather be stuck on a rocketship floating through space or stuck in a boat in the middle of the ocean?

275.   Would you rather have a million dollars in pennies or a hundred million dollars worth of candy?

276.   Would you rather go bungee jumping or skydiving?

277.   Would you rather have a pet dragon or a pet dinosaur?

278.   Would you rather swim in a pool of mud or swim in a pool of pudding?

279.   Would you rather receive a shot from your doctor or get a cavity filled by your dentist?

280.   Would you rather be the fastest swimmer in the world be the second fastest runner in the world?

281.   Would you rather live in a tree house for the rest of your life or live on a boat house for the rest of your life?

282.   Would you rather have a new candy named after you or a newly discovered animal named after you?

283.   Would you rather be the head of secret services for the president or be a superhero that never gains recognition?

284.   Would you rather own a company that no one knows about or work for the most famous company in the world?

285.   Would you rather know the lyrics to every song ever written or be able to speak five different languages?

286.   Would you rather be unable to talk ever again or only be able to speak at a loud volume whenever you speak?

287.   Would you rather have the power to understand animals when they speak but unable for them to understand you, or have the power to speak to animals in their language without being able to understand them in return?

288.   Would you rather have everything you ever wanted and needed given to you or have the money for everything you ever wanted and needed?

289.   Would you rather be able to draw really good or be able to sing really good?

290.   Would you rather be a superhero that no one knows or be a super villain that everyone knows?

291.   Would you rather eat fast food for every meal for the rest of your life or never be able to eat fast food again?

292.   Would you rather be the King/Queen of another country or be the President of the United States?

293.   Would you rather know the correct answer for every test you take or never have to take another test again?

294.   Would you rather be the smartest kid at your school or be the best kid at sports in your school?

295.   Would you rather own 10 puppies or own 10 kittens?

296.   Would you rather travel around the world or travel through time?

297.   Would you rather eat a bowl of worms or eat a single spider?

298.   Would you rather have the power to be invisible or have the power to read people's minds?

299.   Would you rather eat a whole lemon or a whole raw potato?

300.   Would you rather have the ability to fly or have the ability to breathe underwater?

301.   Would you rather have only one best friend for the rest of your life or have 10 best friends that live in other countries?

302.   Would you rather be shrunk down to the size of a bug or become the size of a whale?

303.   Would you rather swim in the ocean with sharks or be stuck in a cage with a lion?

304.   Would you rather be a maid for the dirtiest person in the world or be a chef for someone who eats all day long?

305. **Would you rather take a day trip to the zoo or a day trip to the beach?**

SPEED DIAL QUESTIONS!

Would you rather...

1. **Be a cat or a dog for a day?**

2. **Eat a banana sandwich with mayonnaise or jelly?**

3. **Fall into a mud puddle or fall into yellow snow?**

4. **Get a stain on your shirt or walk into a pole?**

5. Jump into a pool or into a pile of leaves?

6. Leave Play-Doh out to dry or put it away to use again?

7. Wear shoes on the wrong feet or wear someone else's stinky shoes?

8. Get yelled at by mom or dad?

9. Be grounded for a week or be forced to hug your brother/sister for 5 minutes?

10. Live in a treehouse or live in a tent in the woods?

11. Build a pillow fort or a fort out of sheets?

12. Ride a dirtbike or a quad?

13. Be good at an easy sport or stink at a hard sport?

14. Get a flat tire on your bike or have the chain pop off?

15. Down a cup of Kool-Aid or a cup of chocolate milk?

16. Eat a pound of Reeses Peanut Butter Cups or a pound of Skittles?

17. Find a pot of gold or find a pot of money at the end of a rainbow?

18. Tell your crush you like her and be turned down, or never tell your crush you like her and find out she liked you too after it's too late?

19. Have a cat or a dog?

20. Catch a big fish or many little fish?

21. Go camping in the backyard or in the mountains?

22. Sleep in a tent or sleep in a camper?

23. Go potty in a bucket or go potty in the woods?

24. Win an argument or win at Monopoly?

25. Play the guitar or play the violin?

26. Listen to loud music or no music at all?

27. Watch Mickey Mouse Clubhouse or Spongebob Squarepants?

28. Watch a boring adult movie or a baby movie?

29. Read comic books or play Minecraft?

30. Go trick-or-treating or go on an Easter egg hunt?

31. Eat a popsicle or ice cream?

32. It's the middle of the hottest summer ever, would you rather play in sprinklers outside or stay indoors?

33. Play hide and seek or cops and robbers?

34. Play dodgeball or kickball?

35. Get flour in your face or an egg smashed over your head?

36. Smell rotten eggs or your dad's shoes?

37. Eat a hotdog or a hamburger?

38. Eat pizza or McDonalds?

39. Go on a rollercoaster that goes upside-down or go on a ride that spins really fast?

40. Give a high-five or a handshake?

41. Eat a plate of broccoli or eat a salad without dressing?

42. Catch the chicken pox or catch the cooties?

43. Get a shot or be sick for a few days?

44. Eat food from the cafeteria or pack a lunch?

45. Eat peanut butter and jelly for a week or ramen noodles for a week?

46. Dive off the high-dive or be the target for dodge ball practice?

47. Play flag football or tackle football?

48. Go to the movies or have a sleepover?

49. Do the hokey pokey or the chicken dance?

50. Have a runny nose or a stuffy nose?

CONCLUSION

Wow! You made it through all 700 of the questions in *The Would You Rather Book for Kids*. How did you and your friends and family end up doing? Most of these Questions have been around for generations and have special places in countless people's hearts. We hope they had the same effect on you!

Once again, we would like to thank you for reading our book *The Would You Rather Book for Kids* and can't wait to hear what you thought about it. If you enjoyed this book, please don't forget to leave a review and let us know how much you loved it. Reviews mean the world to us and help us continue to create books just like this one for years to come.

Thank you!

Funny Fox

Ps. it would mean the world to us if you could take 30 seconds out of your day and leave us a review! It helps us continue to make books like these and help children around the world enjoy the beautiful art of reading and entertaining.

Printed by Amazon Italia Logistica S.r.l.
Torrazza Piemonte (TO), Italy